THE BRIDE MAKES HERSELF READY

PATRICIA KING

THE BRIDE MAKES HERSELF READY

PREPARING FOR THE LORD'S RETURN

ISBN: 978-1-62166-555-7
Published by Patricia King Enterprises
PatriciaKing.com

PKE

Patricia King Enterprises

For worldwide distribution.

Dedicated to
Jesus Christ,
my Bridegroom King

ACKNOWLEDGMENT

No one on earth has taught me more about love than my husband, Ron. We were married in March 1973 and over the years he has consistently lived in unconditional love.

Thank you Ron, for being you. Thank you for teaching me what it is like to feel "treasured." Thank you for manifesting the love of our Heavenly Bridegroom.

You met me in my time of great despair and saw value that I couldn't see in myself at the time. You loved me to life. "Love lifted me. When nothing else could help, love lifted me"... and your love still does!

TABLE OF CONTENTS

A LOVE STORY

The Bible is a beautiful love story revealing the Father's search for a Bride for His Son. We see the story unfold in the first book of the Bible when the Father spoke concerning Adam, "It is not good for the man to be alone; I will make him a helper suitable for him" (Genesis 2:18).

Throughout the Scriptures we see this theme continue all the way to the final chapters in the Bible, describing this perfect Bride who made herself ready. The Bride longs for her Bridegroom. Her heart is towards Him all day long and she yearns for and calls for His return. The Bible closes with the cry of the Bride: *"The Spirit and the bride say, Come"* (Revelation 22:17).

In the ancient Hebrew wedding tradition we discover a clear analogy of the marriage union of Christ and His Bride. Let's discover together the mystery and glory of the Bride of Christ.

"Who is this coming up from the wilderness leaning on her beloved?"

Song of Solomon 8:5

THE BETROTHAL

In the ancient Hebrew wedding tradition, the father chose the bride for his son. Although the son's desire was considered, his father made the final choice. The son then went to meet the father of the bride to ask him for her hand in marriage. He took three things to present to him:

1. The Bride Price. The young man brought a large sum of gold, silver, jewels, or flocks to offer to the girl's father as the price he was willing to pay to purchase the daughter as his wife. This payment was called the bride price (*Mohar*).

From the time a son was born to a family, the father began to save up the bride price to ensure that his son would have a wife of good stock in the same, or better, socio and economic class, to give him healthy and intelligent children. If the bride price was too small, the bride's father could be offended, as it would reflect the lack of his daughter's value in the eyes of the young man and his family. If offended with an insufficient bride price, he could refuse to give his daughter to him in marriage. Sometimes an insufficient bride price was negotiated and the bride's father would give the groom opportunity to return at a determined time with the negotiated amount. If the bride's father was pleased with the amount, he would officially receive the bride price and they would proceed.

An excellent wife, who can find? For her worth is far above jewels. (Proverbs 31:10)

Jesus paid the extravagant price of His very own life for you. Your Heavenly Father chose you to be His Son's Bride. When Jesus gave His life on the cross and paid the penalty for your sins, He was paying the bride price.

For you have been bought with a price: therefore glorify God in your body. (1 Corinthians 6:20)

You were bought with a price... (1 Corinthians 7:23)

Conduct yourselves in fear during the time of your stay on earth; knowing that you were not redeemed with perishable things like silver or gold ... but with precious blood, as of a lamb unblemished and spotless, the blood of Christ. (1 Peter 1:17-19)

You are so very precious to the Lord. Do you understand your value? You are His "Pearl of Great Price" for which He gave His all to purchase. When He looks at you, His heart is ravished. You are altogether lovely to Him.

2. The Marriage Contract. The Hebrew law (*Torah*), as well as the civil law, included clear instruction and legal responsibilities regarding terms of marriage. In addition to these laws, the groom prepared a written document stating the rights of the bride and his promises to her. The bride's father carefully reviewed each point of the contract. If he was pleased with the terms and agreed to give his daughter to the young man in marriage, he would call for his daughter and wife and share the news of the betrothal. When the bride agreed, her father and the bridegroom would sign the contract.

This document became an official, legal covenant and established the relationship as a betrothal or engagement. The betrothal was much more serious than a marriage engagement today. From the time the covenant contract was signed, the bride and groom were committed as man and wife, although the union was not yet consummated. It was not permitted for them to have sexual relations before the wedding ceremony. Even though the ceremony and the consummation might take place up to two years later, only a certificate of divorce could dissolve the union once the covenant was signed.

The New Testament (and all the promises in the Bible) is your marriage covenant and contract with Jesus.

Grace and peace be multiplied to you in the knowledge of God and of Jesus our Lord; seeing that His divine power has granted to us everything pertaining to life and godliness, through the true knowledge of Him who called us by His own glory and excellence. For by these He has granted to us His precious and magnificent promises, so that by them you may become partakers of the divine nature, having escaped the corruption that is in the world by lust. (2 Peter 1:2-4)

When you understand that the Bible reveals your marriage covenant with your Heavenly Bridegroom, it changes the way you read it. I remember reading the Bible as a young Christian. It was like a love letter from Jesus Himself written personally to me. Every time I read the Word I beheld promises that awakened my spirit. Oh, how wonderful it was to receive fresh words from my Bridegroom each and every day.

Invite the Holy Spirit to open your eyes to your divine marriage covenant revealed within the Scriptures. Every promise is yours. Every blessing is yours. Jesus wants you to know His goodness towards you. He is an amazing Bridegroom and has given you absolutely everything He has.

Paul prayed a prayer for the church at Ephesus that is very powerful. Invite the Holy Spirit to do the same for you.

That the God of our Lord Jesus Christ, the Father of glory, may give to you a spirit of wisdom and of revelation in the knowledge of Him. I pray that the eyes of your heart may be enlightened, so that you will know what is the hope of His calling, what are the riches of the glory of His inheritance in the saints. (Ephesians 1:17-18)

3. The Skin of Wine. The groom brought a skin of wine to the father of the bride for "the cup of acceptance." When the bride price was accepted and the covenant was signed, the father of the bride, along with the groom and his bride, drank the cup of acceptance. In the drinking of the cup the bride committed herself in covenant to the young man. This sealed the betrothal. Immediately a trumpet (*shofar*) sounded to announce the betrothal.

And he (Jesus) took the cup, and gave thanks, and gave it to them, saying, "Drink you all of it; for this is my blood of the new testament, which is shed for many for the remission of sins." (Matthew 26:27-28 KJV)

After the betrothal, the bridegroom prepared to return to his father's house, as they were to be separated for 12 months, and possibly up to two years. They could not see each other without a chaperone during this time. The chaperone, also called the "messenger," brought messages from the bridegroom to his bride and from the bride to her bridegroom. The Holy Spirit is our Chaperone and Messenger. Jesus said He would not leave us alone but would send the Helper (John 14:16-17.)

After the trumpet sounded, the bridegroom presented his bride with gifts before he left so she would not forget him, just as we were given the Holy Spirit's gifts when Jesus left the earth to go to heaven. According to the tradition, as the bridegroom left his bride to return to his father's house, he declared, *"I go and prepare a place for you. I will come again and receive you to myself, that where I am you may be also."*

In John 14:1-3 Jesus explained that He was going to prepare a place in His Father's house and promised to return to "receive you to Myself, that where I am, there you may be also." He was speaking marriage terminology. His disciples would have understood that.

After the bridegroom made this final proclamation, he left his bride to return to his father's house.

I remember the time my husband went away for a three-day fishing trip after we first fell in love. We had been going together for about a month. When he said goodbye to me that morning, I thought my heart was going to break. I missed him from the moment he left, and I wouldn't see him again for three whole days! (We had no cell phones back then.) The entire time he was gone, all I could think of was Ron. He was on my mind when I got up and he was on my mind when I went to bed. He was on my heart all day long. I was truly smitten with love for him. When he returned, he told me he felt the same. He loves fishing trips but he couldn't focus on fishing. All he could think of was me.

This is how Jesus feels about you. He has gone to prepare your bridal chamber. Thoughts of you consume Him. He is lovesick and can hardly wait to come back for you, but He is restrained until the Father releases Him. You have totally captured His heart and His focus.

His Bride's attention is fully captured by Him, too. She is focused on Him, when she wakes up and when she goes to bed. She thinks of Him all day long, not because she has to, but because she is overcome by love. Jesus, her Bridegroom, is her most important focus in life because of her love for Him.

In Mark 14:1-9, we find Mary of Bethany pouring out her alabaster vial of very costly perfume on Jesus. Many believe this was her dowry and her only earthly assurance of ever having a husband. Being married was very important for a young Jewish girl in those days due to the fact that the men were the providers, protectors and covering for the women. It was a disgrace for women of marriageable age to be single or barren. However, due to her deep love for Jesus, she poured out all that represented her future dreams and well-being upon

Him. She poured out her dowry on Him. She didn't care what anyone thought. Others in the room were not at all pleased with what she was doing, but she did not care. She had eyes for only One. Jesus said, "She has done a good deed to Me... Truly, I say to you, wherever the gospel is preached in the whole world, what this woman has done will also be spoken of in memory of her" (Mark 14:6,9).

Bridal love is so beautiful. When you fall in love, it is not a chore to focus – *it is a delight.* You can't help yourself. You don't think, "Oh I better strive and choose to think about the one I love today." This is something that flows from your heart. It is all encompassing. Do you want this kind of love for Jesus, your Bridegroom? Is this something you treasure and desire more than anything in life? If you want it, you can have it. Aggressively pursue your desire to be filled with perfect bridal love. Receive this bridal love by faith and allow the Holy Spirit to transform you. The Lord will grant you the desires of your heart.

Where your treasure is, there your heart will be also. (Matthew 6:21)

Therefore I say to you, all things for which you pray and ask, believe that you have received them, and they will be granted you. (Mark 11:24)

The young Hebrew bride focused on her bridegroom with complete abandonment because she knew he was returning for her. She lived each day, dreaming of her future with him. The investment of the preparation she made in her bridegroom's absence was extremely important for their life together. You always empower what you focus on. If, after he departed, she lived for herself, hung out with her girlfriends and failed to prepare her heart or take care of practical requirements, then she would not be ready for her bridegroom when he returned. How hurtful this would be for him.

The Bride of Christ likewise lives with an eternal perspective. She has "dove's eyes" for Jesus her Bridegroom and prepares for ruling and reigning with Him forever. The love investment made today in preparation for His return definitely affects your eternal future. Jesus is returning for a Bride who is expectantly longing for His return.

THE PREPARATION

THE BRIDEGROOM

The bridegroom returned to his father's house to build a house for his bride. This was usually a chamber (*chador*) built onto his father's house. The chamber was often called the *chuppah* (honeymoon bed). It had to be built to his father's specifications and the groom could not return for his bride until his father released him. The groom's father examined the chamber to make sure it was well-built and prepared with excellence. During this period of separation, the father taught his son how to be a husband, provider, protector and father. The groom's family also prepared for the marriage supper and celebration that was to be held at the father of the groom's house. The son chose his best man and attendants, and had his marriage garments made during this season. When the time was right and the bridegroom was ready, his father sent him to receive his bride.

The Bride

While the groom had returned to his father's house to prepare a place for their life together, the bride also made preparations. She collected her trousseau, made her gown and accessories, chose her attendants and prepared for her new life. The bridal gown was fine linen, bright and clean. It was always white as a sign of purity and virginity. Linen symbolized the gift of righteousness we have now received in Christ.

> It was given to her to clothe herself in fine linen, bright and clean; for the fine linen is the righteous acts of the saints. (Revelation 19:8)

Her mother and the older women taught her to be a wife, mother, pleaser of her husband and keeper of the home. During the betrothal, the bride was completely set apart and consecrated for her husband. She could not have eyes, or affections, for anyone else or anything else. She was set apart for her bridegroom alone.

In western Christianity there is a marked sloppiness in lifestyle, worship and devotion. We often find a "take it or leave it" mindset prevailing in many believers, and they choose a little bit of Jesus and a little bit of this and a little bit of that. If we have not completely set apart our lives for Him yet, we must not delay. He is coming soon. We must live separated unto Him, for He is worthy. The Bride of Christ is in the world but not of it. She lives in relevance with those around her as Jesus did in His days on the earth and, like Him, she does not compromise.

THE TIMING OF THE BRIDEGROOM'S RETURN

In this wedding tradition, no one knew when the bridegroom would return for his bride. In fact, he did not even know. Only his father could determine the time.

Jesus stated, "But of that day and hour no one knows, not even the angels of heaven, nor the Son, but the Father alone." (Matthew 24:36)

The bridegroom talked about the timing of his coming for his bride only with his father. He may have communicated with his bride in secret by the chaperone/messenger concerning the general timing, but she never knew the exact hour and neither did he. There were no engraved invitations to be sent out for the wedding. If people preparing the calendar wanted to reserve a day for the celebration, they had a problem. If anyone were to ask the groom when he was coming for his bride, he would inform them by saying, "My father alone knows."

Jesus left the earth to prepare your place in the Father's House as His Bride. He is coming back for you. The day and the hour you do not know, but *you must be ready.*

In the Hebrew wedding tradition, if the bridegroom were to return for his bride and find her ill-prepared, or if she was giving her affections to other things, or another man, it was terms for divorcement and the wedding would be called off. We must be prepared and wholeheartedly anticipating Christ's return. The bride, therefore, had to be in a state of *constant readiness* lest the bridegroom's arrival catch her by surprise. Often she kept a light burning in the window and an extra jar of oil on hand, lest the bridegroom came in the night and found her unprepared.

> Let us rejoice and be glad and give the glory to Him, for the marriage of the Lamb has come and His bride has made herself ready. (Revelation 19:7)

LIKE A THIEF IN THE NIGHT

In the marriage tradition, without notice the bridegroom usually returned at night for his bride. We are taught in the Scriptures that Jesus will come back like a thief in the night, at a time when we do not expect.

> For you yourselves know full well that the day of the Lord will come just like a thief in the night. (1 Thessalonians 5:2)

> Therefore be on the alert, for you do not know which day your Lord is coming. For this reason

you also must be ready; for the Son of Man is coming at an hour when you do not think He will. (Matthew 24:42, 44)

The parable of the ten virgins speaks of the importance of our readiness for that day.

Then the kingdom of heaven will be comparable to ten virgins, who took their lamps and went out to meet the bridegroom. Five of them were foolish, and five were prudent. For when the foolish took their lamps, they took no oil with them, but the prudent took oil in flasks along with their lamps. Now while the bridegroom was delaying, they all got drowsy and began to sleep. But at midnight there was a shout, "Behold, the bridegroom! Come out to meet him." Then all those virgins rose and trimmed their lamps. The foolish said to the prudent, 'Give us some of your oil, for our lamps are going out.' But the prudent answered, "No, there will not be enough for us and you too; go instead to the dealers and buy some for yourselves." And while they were going away to make the purchase, the bridegroom came, and those who were ready went in with him to the wedding feast; and the door was shut. Later the other virgins also came, saying, "Lord, lord, open up for us." But he answered, "Truly I say to you, I do not know you." Be on the alert then, for you do not know the day nor the hour. (Matthew 25:1-13)

In this parable there were ten virgins with a number of things in common:

1. They were all expecting the bridegroom.

2. They all had lamps.

3. They all heard the shout at midnight.

4. They all went out to meet him.

There was one significant difference: five of them were ready and five of them were not.

The five that lacked fresh oil for their lamps ran to get it at the last minute but it was too late. When they came to the wedding feast later, after they bought their oil, the door was already shut. They cried out, "Lord, Lord, open up for us." He replied, "I do not know you."

The Bride of Christ is a wise virgin. She awaits her Bridegroom with oil in her lamp.

In Scripture, "oil" represents the anointing of the Holy Spirit who comes and fills us to overflowing with His Presence. The easiest way to be filled is simply to spend time with the Lord. We see a picture of this in Psalm 23. The Lord welcomes us to His banqueting table where we meet with Him in intimate communion. As we do, the Word says He pours out His oil upon us until we overflow like a cup that has been filled beyond its brim (Psalm 23:5).

To make sure you are full of fresh oil, spend time with God. Here are three simple ways you can do that every day:

1. Read Your Bible! Scripture is more than print on a page, it is the Living Heart of God revealed. As you get into the Word, the Word gets into you – filling you with His Truth until you overflow with Him everywhere you go!

2. Worship! When we praise the Lord we are turning our hearts to Him, drawing near to declare our love and appreciation of what He has done, and of who He is. In James 4:8 the Lord promises that as we draw near to Him, He will draw near to us. When we praise and worship, it is like singing an enthusiastic "Yes!" to the invitation of Psalm 23 to come and sit with Him. We cannot help but be filled with His presence!!

3. Pray! Any good relationship is built from good communication. Prayer is talking with God, sharing your heart with Him and taking the time to let Him share His heart with you. Like with worship, to talk with God is to draw near to God. When we do, He draws near to us – filling us afresh with His presence. When we turn to the Lord in prayer we become like

John the Beloved, leaning against the breast of Jesus. So close. So intimate, we can hear the very beating of His heart, that glorious heart of His that beats for each and every one of us!

CALLED AND CHOSEN

The parable of the marriage feast:

The kingdom of heaven may be compared to a king who gave a wedding feast for his son. And he sent out his slaves to call those who had been invited to the wedding feast, and they were unwilling to come. Again he sent out other slaves saying, "Tell those who have been invited, 'Behold, I have prepared my dinner; my oxen and my fattened livestock are all butchered and everything is ready; come to the wedding feast.'" But they paid no attention and went their way, one to his own farm, another to his business, and the rest seized his slaves and mistreated them and killed them. But the king was enraged, and he sent his armies and destroyed those murderers and set their city on fire. Then he said to his slaves, "The wedding is ready, but those who were invited were not worthy. Go therefore to the main highways and as many as you find there, invite to the wedding feast." Those slaves went out in the streets and gathered together all they found, both evil and good; and the wedding hall was filled with dinner guests. But when the king came in to look over the dinner guests, he saw a man there who was not dressed in wedding clothes, and he said to him, "Friend, how did you come in here without wedding clothes?" And the man was speechless.

Then the king said to the servants, "Bind him hand and foot, and throw him into the outer darkness; in that place there will be weeping and gnashing of teeth." For many are called, but few are chosen. (Matthew 22:2-14)

Every believer is called to the wedding but only those who are prepared are chosen. Those who love Him will prepare. These desire more than anything to prepare for Him because He is their focus. They want nothing more in life than to draw close to Him. They love Him more than life itself.

If you can identify a desire for this, pray and ask the Holy Spirit to prepare you as the Bride of Christ. I cannot stress this enough. The Lord will give you the desires of your heart. You might not feel passion for Jesus, but it doesn't mean you don't have it. Identify your deepest longing. Is it to know Him? Is it to be fully abandoned to Him? Is it to be His Bride? If these things are your desire, you can have them all. The Father looks at your heart. He knows you completely and intimately. Cry out to Him and ask Him to fill you with fresh love for your Bridegroom. Invite Him to fill you with a heart of complete focus. If this is truly your desire, His grace will accomplish it for you. Run after your desire. You can have it. You can. You will!

THE MARRIAGE CEREMONY

When the father informed his son that it was time to receive his bride, he dressed in his wedding garments and called for his best man and attendants. His family and friends also got ready. The best man, along with the other attendants, went slightly ahead of the groom and blew a trumpet (*shofar*). This was called "the last trump." The best man then shouted, *"Behold the bridegroom. Come out to meet him!"*

At that time the bride and her attendants quickly dressed. If they were sleeping, the moment they heard the blast of the trumpet and the call to meet the bridegroom they jumped out of bed and prepared immediately. Often the attendants (who were sometimes younger sisters and cousins) stayed in the bride's room during the final months while she waited for her bridegroom. They had the bride's garments, jewels, fragrances, and everything needed for the wedding, ready and waiting to go. All their lamps were trimmed and filled with fresh oil.

When the trumpet sounded, the entire village rose to celebrate and, along with the bride and her attendants, ran out to meet the bridegroom. The bridegroom passionately "caught up" his bride and took her to his father's house. There was great celebration and joy with shouts, blasts of trumpets, singing and dancing.

The father of the groom was ready for the celebration. The groom's family and friends were already at the father's house waiting for the other guests and the arrival of the bride and groom. The bride's guests, friends and attendants went ahead to the father's house, followed directly by the bride and groom.

THE CORONATION

The bride was veiled when her groom came for her and she remained veiled during the wedding. On their arrival, the groom's father took the hand of the bride and placed it in the hand of his son. Crowns were then placed on both the bride's and groom's heads. They were called the king and queen during the celebration. This was in reference to the *Feast of Trumpets*.

And when the Chief Shepherd appears, you will receive the unfading crown of glory. (1 Peter 5:4)

The biblical festival, *Feast of Trumpets* (*Rosh Hasha-nah*), is known as the first day of the Jewish calendar year and refers to the Wedding of the Messiah to His Bride. It is also known as the *Coronation of the Messiah.*

There are seven feasts listed in the Bible. Four of them are spring feasts and three of them are celebrated in the fall. All the biblical spring feasts were fulfilled at Christ's first coming on the exact days of the feasts. The fall feasts speak of His second coming. The *Feast of Pentecost* (the last spring feast of the year) prophesied the commencing of the church age. This was fulfilled in history on the actual day of Pentecost, around 2000 years ago.

For those who believe in the rapture of the church, the *Feast of Trumpets* (the next feast in the Jewish Calendar and the first fall feast) signals the Second Advent as Jesus returns to rapture His Bride. This will end the church age and begin the Kingdom age. It signifies the beginning of Christ's rule as King. Many believe this will also mark the beginning of the seven years of tribulation for those left on the earth.

In a moment, in the twinkling of an eye, at the last trumpet; for the trumpet will sound, and the dead will be raised imperishable, and we will be changed. (1 Corinthians 15:52)

For the Lord Himself will descend from heaven with a shout, with the voice of the archangel and with the trumpet of God, and the dead in Christ will rise first. Then we who are alive and remain will be caught up together with them in the clouds to meet the Lord in the air, and so we shall always be with the Lord. (1 Thessalonians 4:16-17)

THE CONSUMMATION

After being crowned, the groom and his veiled bride were escorted to the bridal chamber (*chuppah*). They entered alone to consummate the marriage. When the marriage was consummated, the groom announced the consummation to the other members of the wedding party waiting outside the chamber. The guests, families and attendants then cheered and celebrated.

He who has the bride is the bridegroom; but the friend of the bridegroom, who stands and hears him, rejoices greatly because of the bridegroom's voice. (John 3:29)

The marriage celebration, held in the groom's father's house, lasted seven days. It is possible that the seven days represents the seven years of tribulation[1] on

---

[1] Jesus spoke of a tribulation such as the earth has never known (Matthew 24:21). Eschatologists have various convictions regarding the actual time and endurance of this period. Most believe the Tribulation will last seven years, based on Daniel 9:24-27, whereas the Great Tribulation, the last half of the Tribulation, will last three and half years (Revelation 11:3).

the earth at which time the raptured Bride is in the heavenly chuppah with her Bridegroom. During the wedding tradition, the newly married couple spent seven days alone together in sexual intimacy, getting to know each other and planning their life together.

I realize there are a variety of interpretations and summaries of Bible eschatology. There are many views on the rapture, or lack of rapture, and numerous perspectives on if the rapture is before, during or after the tribulation. I have reviewed many a thesis and points of views on these subjects over the years and they all include great arguments for consideration. At the end of the day we have to agree on one thing, "GOD KNOWS!"

For me, the main deliberation is that we completely commit to love the Lord our God with all our hearts, with all our minds and with all our strength, at all times. I made a decision long ago to follow the Lord fully, in good times or in difficult times. If I am in the midst of a cruel tribulation, I want my love for God to be as passionate as it would be if I were standing before Him in heaven. No one should ever live with an escape mentality but should occupy until He comes, living each day fully for Him. He is watching and knows our hearts. He is the all-wise God, has the entire end-time issue all taken care of, and is not at all worried or concerned!

It is possible that there will be a rapture of the Bride of Christ that parallels the ancient Hebrew wedding tradition. In this case, our Heavenly Bridegroom will come and receive us. We will be caught up to be with Him in heaven for a seven-year period. After that time we will come with Him, and His angel armies, to judge the nations, establish His victory and rule on the earth.

It is also possible that we will not be raptured but will glorify our Lord by living out our unfailing commitment in the midst of the greatest tribulation the world has ever known. There are many other possibilities proposed by those who study Bible eschatology. Again, the main point: live your life for Him in full abandonment, passion and focus each and every day of your life. He is worthy!

With that being said, it appears to me that there are two comings of the Lord to examine. One is the return for His Bride where she will be *caught up... to meet the Lord in the air*" (1 Thessalonians 4:16-17). There is evidence in Scripture that suddenly believers will disappear from the earth during this time.

And He will send forth His angels with A GREAT TRUMPET and THEY WILL GATHER TO-GETHER His elect from the four winds, from one end of the sky to the other (Matthew 24:31).

But of that day and hour no one knows, not even the angels of heaven, nor the Son, but the Father alone. For the coming of the Son of Man will be just like the days of Noah. For as in those days before the flood they were eating and drinking, marrying and giving in marriage, until the day that Noah entered the ark, and they did not understand until the flood came and took them all away; so will the coming of the Son of Man be. Then there will be two men in the field; one will be taken and one will be left. Two women will be grinding at the mill; one will be taken and one will be left. Therefore be on the alert, for you do not know which day your Lord is coming. (Matthew 24:36-42)

The second return is indicated in the Scriptures when Jesus will come back out of heaven to the earth to judge and establish His Kingdom (Revelation 19:11-21).

But when the Son of Man comes in His glory, and all the angels with Him, then He will sit on His glorious throne. All the nations will be gathered before Him; and He will separate them from one another, as the shepherd separates the sheep from the goats; and He will put the sheep on His right, and the goats on the left. Then the King will say to those on His right, "Come, you who are blessed of My Father, inherit the kingdom prepared for you from the foundation of the world."

Then He will also say to those on His left, "Depart from Me, accursed ones, into the eternal fire which has been prepared for the devil and his angels." (Matthew 25:31-34, 41)

It is possible that the seven days the bride and groom are in the chamber of intimacy in heaven represents the seven years where the Bride of Christ is removed from the earth and caught up to be with her Bridegroom.

It is interesting that from the last day of the two-day *Feast of Trumpets* (Coronation/Rosh Hashanah) to the day before Yom Kippur (the Day of Atonement) is seven days.

According to Jewish custom, three books were opened on the *Feast of Trumpets*:

1. The Book of Life for the righteous

2. The Book of Life for the unrighteous

3. The Book of Life for those who were in the balance

Just prior to the *Feast of Trumpets*, a person's life and works were evaluated from the previous year. If an individual was deemed righteous, their name was written in the Book of Life for the righteous. If an individual was deemed unrighteous, their name would be written in the Book of Life for the unrighteous and they would not survive the year. If an individual was weighed in the balance, then judgment was delayed until Yom Kippur. This gave them seven days[2] from the end of Trumpets (Rosh Hashanah) until Yom Kippur (Day of Atonement) to repent, align with God's ways and have the judgment of God turned to their favor.

The prophetic significance of the Day of Atonement concerns the physical return of Christ to the earth in glory to bring judgment and to establish His domain for the millennial rule of Christ with His Bride. Perhaps there is symbolism in regard to the books that were opened during Rosh Hashanah. If considering this as an analogous parallel, then those who are "weighed in the balance" would have seven years during the great tribulation to repent, align and have the judgment turned in their favor when Jesus returns to the earth to judge and make war. If this turns out to be the case, I would rather have my name written in the Book of Life for the righteous than have the

---

2 The ten days starting with Rosh Hashanah and ending with Yom Kippur are commonly known as the Days of Awe (Yamim Noraim) or the Days of Repentance. This is a time for serious introspection, a time to consider the sins of the previous year and repent before Yom Kippur. The seven days mentioned in this book are the seven days beginning at the end of Rosh Hashanah after the books are opened and ending the day before Yom Kippur.

opportunity for seven years of tribulation to perfect me, wouldn't you?

And I saw heaven opened, and behold, a white horse, and He who sat on it is called Faithful and True, and in righteousness He judges and wages war. His eyes are a flame of fire, and on His head are many diadems; and He has a name written on Him which no one knows except Himself. He is clothed with a robe dipped in blood, and His name is called The Word of God. And the armies which are in heaven, clothed in fine linen, white and clean, were following Him on white horses. From His mouth comes a sharp sword, so that with it He may strike down the nations, and He will rule them with a rod of iron; and He treads the wine press of the fierce wrath of God, the Almighty. And on His robe and on His thigh He has a name written, "KING OF KINGS, AND LORD OF LORDS." (Revelation 19:11-16)

THE PRESENTATION

On the seventh day the best man waited at the door of the chuppah. The groom knocked when they were ready. The doors of the chuppah were opened by the best man. The groom, with his now unveiled bride, came forth and they were presented as man and wife before the guests. From this time on, they officially and publicly lived their lives together, ruling and reigning over their domain of influence and building their family.

RULING AND REIGNING WITH JESUS FOREVER

The marriage covenant between Christ and His Bride is an eternal, unbreakable covenant. Jesus will not have more than one wife. He is marrying a Bride who has made herself ready, a Bride who has eyes only for Him. He is marrying a Bride who wants nothing else in life but to know Him, to be intimate with Him, to live with Him and serve Him forever. He is marrying a Bride who does not love the world or the things of the world. She is fully separated unto Him and Him alone. She loves the things He loves and hates the things He hates. This is the heart of the Bride of Christ. Jesus will rule and reign with His Bride for eternity.

What does this Bride look like? The Bride is pure and holy as He is pure and holy. She is patient and kind. She is gentle and meek. She is submissive, obedient and full of courage. She is industrious and resourceful. She is faithful and full of faith. She is beautiful beyond description and magnificent in glory.

The Bride's glory is described in Scripture as the New Jerusalem in heaven, perfect in every way. She comes down to the earth from heaven.

And I saw the holy city, new Jerusalem, coming down out of heaven from God, made ready as a bride adorned for her husband. (Revelation 21:2)

Then one of the seven angels who had the seven bowls full of the seven last plagues came and spoke with me, saying, "Come here, I will show you the bride, the wife of the Lamb." And he carried me away in the Spirit to a great and high mountain, and showed me the holy city, Jerusalem, coming down out of heaven from God, having the glory of God. Her brilliance was like a very costly stone, as a stone of crystal-clear jasper. It had a great and high wall, with twelve gates, and at the gates twelve angels; and names were written on them, which are the names of the twelve tribes of the sons of Israel. There were three gates on the east and three gates on the north and three gates on the south and three gates on the west. And the wall of the city had twelve foundation stones, and on them were the twelve names of the twelve apostles of the Lamb. The one who spoke with me had a gold measuring rod to measure the city, and its gates and its wall. The city is laid out as a square, and its length is as great as the width; and he measured the city with the rod, fifteen hundred miles; its length and width and height are equal. And he measured its wall, seventy-two yards, according to human measurements, which are also angelic measurements. The material of the wall was jasper; and the city was pure gold, like clear glass. The foundation stones of the city wall were adorned with every kind of precious stone. The first foundation stone was jasper; the second, sapphire; the third, chalcedony; the fourth, emerald; the fifth, sardonyx; the sixth, sardius; the seventh, crysolite; the eighth, beryl; the ninth, topaz; the tenth, chrysoprase; the eleventh, jacinth; the twelfth, amethyst. And the twelve gates were twelve pearls; each one of the gates was a single pearl. And the street of the city was pure gold, like transparent glass.

I saw no temple in it, for the Lord God the Almighty and the Lamb are its temple. And the city has no need of the sun or of the moon to shine on it, for the glory of God has illumined it, and its lamp is the Lamb. The nations will walk by its light, and the kings of the earth will bring their glory into it. In the daytime (for there will be no night there) its gates will never be closed; and they will bring the glory and the honor of the nations into it; and nothing unclean, and no one who practices abomination and lying, shall ever come into it, but only those whose names are written in the Lamb's book of life. (Revelation 21:9-27)

THE BRIDE

THE NATURE AND CHARACTERISTICS

OF THE BRIDE OF CHRIST

The Bride loves her Bridegroom with all her heart, mind and strength (Deuteronomy 6:5-6).

1. The Bride is single in her focus and has affections for no other (Exodus 20:3-4).

2. The Bride is submissive, meek, obedient and yielded to her Bridegroom (1 Peter 3:4-6).

3. The Bride has purified herself and made herself ready (Revelation 19:7).

4. The Bride produces righteous acts (Revelation 19:8).

5. The Bride is virtuous, industrious, trustworthy, courageous, faithful and God-fearing (Proverbs 31:10-31).

6. The Bride passionately seeks her Bridegroom and is filled with fresh oil – the Holy Spirit (Matthew 25:4).

7. The Bride longs for the return of her Bridegroom and is alert and watching (1 John 3:2-3).

8. The Bride is glorious without spot, wrinkle, blemish or any such thing (Ephesians 5:22-29).

9. The Bride is an overcomer (Revelation 2 and 3 – overcomes the issues brought up in the seven letters to the churches).

WHO IS THE BRIDE?

We have read about the ancient Hebrew wedding tradition and the Scriptures regarding the analogous parallels to the marriage of the Lamb of God and His Bride. But who exactly is the Bride? Yes, the Bride is the New Jerusalem coming out of heaven, but does she include you? Does she include me?

Some state that the Bride of Christ is made up of all believers. Others are convinced the Bride includes the Jews who have received the Messiah. Some believe that the Bride is made up of Christians living at the time of the rapture and yet others are convinced the Bride is a consecrated remnant within the Body who are waiting for the return of the Lord.

I am certain the Lord wants His Bride to include all believers, yet I personally do not sense that all will be included in His Bride. God alone knows the heart of each individual. He knows if your heart is completely His or not. The Scripture clearly teaches that the Bride of Christ "makes herself ready." She will have a heart only for Him. This single heart focus is the main quality of the Bride.

My personal conviction is that the Bride is a remnant within the Body of believers who is completely consecrated unto the Bridegroom and who is obedient to His Word. Those in this remnant have made themselves ready by watching over their hearts with all diligence. They love and serve Him in complete abandonment, are not legalistic or religious in their motivation, and neither are they bound by self-righteousness. They live with this focus of complete abandonment *because* they love Him. They believe the truth about Him and know He is worthy and deserving of their all. They obey Him *because* they love Him.

"If you love Me, you will keep My commandments." (John 14:15)

"If you keep My commandments, you will abide in My love; just as I have kept My Father's commandments and abide in His love. These things I have spoken to you so that My joy may be in you, and that your joy may be made full." (John 15:10-11)

I know many who believe that Jesus is Lord, have received Him by faith as their personal Savior and yet their hearts are far from Him in their daily lives. They still rule their own life and give very little place to the Lord's ways and direction. They deliberately continue in sinful practices they know are forbidden in Scripture and do not even seem to be concerned about it. Churches are full of those who gaze on pornography, commit fornication and adultery, are involved in homosexuality, have abortions, get drunk, abuse drugs, and who lie, cheat and steal. We could add many more predominant, sinful practices found in the church, such as pride, gossip, unforgiveness, slander and disobedience to the great commission, but enough has been mentioned to paint the picture.

I know many Christians who confess they love and serve the Lord, yet they love the world and its lusts. In Paul's letters, the Apostle of Grace constantly exhorted believers to live godly and run the race (of their lives) as to win the prize. He also spoke of the danger of disqualification. I believe he was speaking of the prize of being the Bride (1 Corinthians 9:24-27).

In Rick Joyner's book, *The Final Quest*, he envisioned various positions in heaven that were assigned to believers according to devotion and service. All who were in heaven were happy to be there, even the ones on the outer fringes, but many had remorse for not serving the Lord fully during their time on the earth. They were positioned for eternity depending on the fruit of their lives while on the earth. The Bride's heart is revealed, tested and proven while she is on the earth. When our lives are terminated in the realm of time, or if Jesus comes when we do not expect Him, there are no more opportunities to obtain our reward. The rewards in Rick Joyner's vision were described as positions before the Lord in heaven. He saw many very close to the Lord and His throne, but also multitudes afar off on the outer fringes. The ones on the outer fringes that failed to obtain the "prize" had remorse for not serving the Lord fully on the earth. They did not have another opportunity once their time on earth was completed.

Paul understood the importance of sowing his life for the gospel while on the earth. He spoke of an eternal reward.

Brethren, I do not regard myself as having laid hold of it yet; but one thing I do: forgetting what lies behind and reaching forward to what lies ahead, I press on toward the goal for the prize of the upward call of God in Christ Jesus. (Philippians 3:13-14)

But without faith it is impossible to please him: for he that cometh to God must believe that he is, and that he is a rewarder of them that diligently seek him. (Hebrews 11:6 KJV)

The Scripture gives clear instruction on all issues of life and godliness. We are to embrace the full counsel of God. If you read through your Scriptures methodically, and believe every word, it will transform you and keep you in the truth. Your spirit will rejoice with the truth, for both the Spirit and the Word are in agreement. Read the following Scriptures carefully and believe each word. Don't read these portions lightly or skim over them. These Scriptures are the Word of God and they will help align you to His ways and prepare you as His Bride.

Do not love the world nor the things in the world. If anyone loves the world, the love of the Father is not in him. For all that is in the world, the lust of the flesh and the lust of the eyes and the boastful pride of life, is not from the Father, but is from the world. The world is passing away, and also its lusts; but the one who does the will of God lives forever. (1 John 2:15-17)

For where your treasure is, there your heart will be also. The eye is the lamp of the body; so then if your eye is clear, your whole body will be full of light. But if your eye is bad, your whole body will be full of darkness. If then the light that is in you is darkness, how great is the darkness! No one can serve two masters; for either he will hate the one and love the other, or he will be devoted to one and despise the other. You cannot serve God and wealth. (Matthew 6:21-24)

Then the Lord said, "...this people draw near with their words and honor Me with their lip service, but they remove their hearts far from Me." (Isaiah 29:13)

Watch over your heart with all diligence, for from it flow the springs of life. (Proverbs 4:23)

You adulteresses, do you not know that friendship with the world is hostility toward God? Therefore whoever wishes to be a friend of the world makes himself an enemy of God. (James 4:4)

For speaking out arrogant words of vanity they entice by fleshly desires, by sensuality, those who barely escape from the ones who live in error, promising them freedom while they themselves are slaves of corruption; for by what a man is overcome, by this he is enslaved. For if, after they have escaped the defilements of the world by the knowledge of the Lord and Savior Jesus Christ, they are again entangled in them and are overcome, the last state has become worse for them than the first. (2 Peter 2:18-20)

For it would be better for them not to have known the way of righteousness, than having known it, to turn away from the holy commandment handed on to them. It has happened to them according to the true proverb, "A dog returns to its own vomit," and, "A sow, after washing, returns to wallowing in the mire." (2 Peter 2:21-22)

These Scriptures do not sound like the Lord is welcoming such followers to be His Bride. Paul, in his letter to the church at Ephesus, described the parallel between the marriage of a man and a woman and Christ's relationship to His church.

Husbands, love your wives, just as Christ also loved the church and gave Himself up for her, so that He might sanctify her, having cleansed her by the washing of water with the word, that He might present to Himself the church in all her glory, having no spot or wrinkle or any such thing; but that she would be holy and blameless. (Ephesians 5:25-27)

STRONG CONVICTION OF SIN IS A GOOD SIGN

The Scripture clearly states, *"His bride has made **herself** ready"* (Revelation 19:7). It does not say that her Heavenly Father makes her ready, or even His Holy

Spirit. We are not required to achieve our own perfection ... in fact, we can't. Even our best efforts to be perfect enough for our Bridegroom would fall short of His holiness. Our own personal attempts to achieve righteousness and win His favor are the working of a religious mindset and are self-righteous in nature. Jesus is the One who sanctifies and cleanses us, and He gives His righteousness as a gift to us, *but He does so when our hearts are fully towards Him.* He looks for hearts who long for Him and who trust Him to perfect that which concerns them. Our preparation as the Bride begins with the undivided focus and posture of our heart towards Jesus. *The preparation of the Bride is all about the heart.*

If you are troubled and strongly convicted when you do wrong, that is a good sign. It means you are uncomfortable with sin and your heart is leaning towards God. If you didn't love Him so much, you probably wouldn't really care if you sinned. It is not beneficial, or of the Spirit, however, to wallow in self-condemnation, guilt and shame. The identification of holy conviction is good and should never be shunned or ignored. Allow the conviction to go deep.

I remember once ministering to a woman who had committed adultery. I was with her and her friend when she confessed. I was quiet for a moment and then she burst into tears and cried out, "I feel so bad, I feel so bad." Her friend immediately went to comfort her and said, "It's okay. It's not a problem. God loves you." I replied, "Please, let her feel the full impact of her sin. Let her feel the weight of it. Don't comfort too soon." She had been in the affair for two years but had not felt true remorse until that moment. The affair had lost its pleasure and she felt trapped, but not fully repentant or remorseful. As she continued to cry and wail, the conviction of the Spirit entered her and His truth went deeper and deeper like a sword into her soul. She finally saw her selfishness clearly for the first time. She saw the damage that was done to her husband, her children, her church, her friends, and to herself. She saw the pain she caused the man she had the affair with, and the pain she caused his family. Most importantly she felt how she had broken the Lord's heart. It was good for her to feel and experience the full impact of her sin. In this way, she was able to receive the full impact of the mercy of God following.

It is important to feel conviction and to allow the Lord to bring alignment and cleansing. If, however, you are comfortable with sin and think, "Oh well, God doesn't really care and He loves me anyway so I will continue on in sin," then you might be in for a rude awakening. This is a sign that your heart is not for Him. Let's look at some more Scriptures. Again, I exhort you to take your time and read through each verse soberly.

Do not be deceived, God is not mocked; for whatever a man sows, this he will also reap. For the one who sows to his own flesh will from the flesh reap corruption, but the one who sows to the Spirit will from the Spirit reap eternal life (Galatians 6:7-8).

He who overcomes will inherit these things, and I will be his God and he will be My son. But for the cowardly and unbelieving and abominable and murderers and immoral persons and sorcerers and idolaters and all liars, their part will be in the lake that burns with fire and brimstone, which is the second death. (Revelation 21:7-8)

For certain persons have crept in unnoticed ... ungodly persons who turn the grace of our God into licentiousness ... Now I desire to remind you ... that the Lord, after saving a people out of the land of Egypt, subsequently destroyed those who did not believe. And angels who did not keep their own domain, but abandoned their proper abode, He has kept in eternal bonds under darkness for the judgment of the great day, just as Sodom and Gomorrah and the cities around them, since they in the same way as these indulged in gross immorality and went after strange flesh, are exhibited as an example in undergoing the punishment of eternal fire. It was also about these men that Enoch, in the seventh generation from Adam, prophesied, saying, "Behold, the Lord came with many thousands of His holy ones, to execute judgment upon all, and to convict all the ungodly of all their ungodly deeds which they have done in an ungodly way, and of all the harsh things which ungodly sinners have spoken against Him." These are grumblers, finding fault, following after their own lusts; they speak arrogantly, flattering people for the sake of gaining an advantage. (Jude 1:4-7, 14-16)

But you, beloved, ought to remember the words that were spoken beforehand by the apostles of our Lord Jesus Christ, that they were saying to you, "In the last time there will be mockers, following after their own ungodly lusts." These are the ones who cause divisions, worldly-minded, devoid of the Spirit. (Jude 1:17-19)

Or do you not know that the unrighteous will not inherit the kingdom of God? Do not be deceived; neither fornicators, nor idolaters, nor adulterers, nor effeminate, nor homosexuals, nor thieves, nor the covetous, nor drunkards, nor revilers, nor swindlers, will inherit the kingdom of God. (1 Corinthians 6:9-10)

For this you know with certainty, that no immoral or impure person or covetous man, who is an idolater, has an inheritance in the kingdom of Christ and God. Let no one deceive you with empty words, for because of these things the wrath of God comes upon all sons of disobedience. (Ephesians 5:5-6)

This is the judgment, that the Light has come into the world, and men loved the darkness rather than the Light, for their deeds were evil. For everyone who does evil hates the Light, and does not come to the Light for fear that his deeds will be exposed. But he who practices the truth comes to the Light, so that his deeds may be manifested as having been wrought in God. (John 3:19-21)

Not everyone who says to Me, "Lord, Lord," will enter the kingdom of heaven, but he who does the will of My Father who is in heaven will enter. Many will say to Me on that day, "Lord, Lord, did we not prophesy in Your name, and in Your name cast out demons, and in Your name perform many miracles?" And then I will declare to them, "I never knew you; DEPART FROM ME, YOU WHO PRACTICE LAWLESSNESS." (Matthew 7: 21-23)

No Fear

The Bride is not full of fear trying desperately not to sin. In fact, she is not at all sin conscious. She is focused on righteousness and on the love she has for her

Bridegroom. She does not strive. She is at rest. She is in love and consumed by love.

Imagine a woman engaged to a man who is head-over-heels in love with her. She loves and admires him, but all day long she struggles with fear. She questions, *What if I lust after another man and fail to be faithful to my fiancé? What am I going to do?*

Fearful thoughts like these don't even enter the mind of one who is in love. Perfect love casts out all fear.

Some are afraid they are not good enough, or perfect enough, for Jesus. Remember, you were chosen by your Heavenly Father to be the Bride for His Son. He did not choose you because you were perfect. He chose you because He loves you. When you give your life to Christ, He changes you from the inside out.

The Bride of Christ is not full of fear and self-effort. Her love for her Bridegroom flows out of pure joy and expectation. She thinks of her Bridegroom all day long but not because she has to. She is free from all legalistic pressure. She serves and obeys the Lord because she loves Him.

MAKE YOURSELF READY

"His bride has made herself ready."
(Revelation 19:7).

1. **To be the Bride of Christ, you must be born again (John 3:4-18).**

   Invite Jesus Christ into your heart to be your personal Savior and Lord. Ask Him to forgive your sins and give you a brand new life in Him. We are saved by grace through faith and not of works (Ephesians 2:8). Believe that Jesus is Lord and personally receive Him through your faith. He then begins a work within you. He is at work within you both to will and to do of His good pleasure (Philippians 2:13). He is the author and finisher of your faith (Hebrews 12:2).

2. **Dedicate your entire being (spirit, soul and body) to Him.**

   This is how you set yourself apart as the Bride. When you do this, you choose to live for Him alone and He will keep you. This process of dedication and consecration is not just a one-time prayer but a daily commitment that is made from your heart in joy. Remind yourself frequently when you rise, throughout your day and when you go to bed at night, that your life is His and His alone (1 Thessalonians 5:5).

3. **Be filled with the Holy Spirit.**
   The Holy Spirit is your Helper to prepare you as the Bride of Christ. He will give you everything you need and teach you everything you need to know. Oil in the Scripture represents the Holy Spirit and His anointing. The presence of the Holy Spirit grants you fresh oil for your lamp (Acts 1:8; John 14:16-17; 16:8-15; Ephesians 5:18-19).

4. **Invite the Lord to convict and purify your heart and make you holy as He is holy.**
   Repent from any unconfessed sin and receive forgiveness. He will make you holy in all your behavior and actions when you ask Him with sincere desire and faith. His grace is available to influence you to be just like Him (Matthew 5:48).

5. **Abstain from every form of evil.**
   Make right choices for Him every day. Live with an eternal perspective (1 Thessalonians 5:21-22). Ask

the Lord to keep you from temptation and deliver you from evil (Matthew 6:13).

6. **Read the Word of God regularly.**
   The Scriptures will make you wise and will be a lamp unto your feet and a light unto your path. Invite the Holy Spirit to reveal the heart of the Bridegroom through the Scriptures. It is His love letter to you (Psalm 119:105).

7. **By faith commune with your Bridegroom and draw close to Him.**
   Worship Him. Listen for Him to speak. By faith receive greater measures of His tender love for you each day (Song of Solomon 2:14). Soak in His love. We love Him because He first loved us (1 John 4:19). Take time to meditate on that love. Drink deep of His love for you (John 7:37).

8. **Perform righteous acts.**
   This is the fruit of your love and faith (James 2:18-20).

9. **Identify yourself as Christ's Bride whom He is ravished over.**
   If you think like a bride, you will act as a bride. As a man thinks in his heart so is he (Proverbs 23:7).

10. Eagerly look for His coming.

When you look for His appearing, you purify yourself just as He is pure (1 John 3:2-3).

ARE YOU READY?

"Soon and very soon we are going to see the King." All the signs are in place and Jesus could return for His Bride at any time. Are you ready? Remember, the Bride makes herself ready. No one can do it for you. You are the one who chooses to turn your heart towards Him fully. If this is your desire, then He will empower you with great grace to accomplish what concerns you. He delights in giving you the desires of your heart (Psalm 37:4).

He loves you so deeply and looks forward to having you with Him as His Bride forever. He paid the extravagant bride price for you. He signed the covenant of His promises with His own blood for you. He is right now preparing the bridal chamber for you.

There is not much time left. Make every moment count. The choices you make now determine many things in your eternal future. What is important to you right now? These are the things you will give yourself to. Live with eternity in your heart. Choices determine your path and outcome in life.

Jacob and Esau were two brothers in the Old Testament. Esau was called to be in the lineage of Christ but he sold his birthright as the eldest son for a single meal (Genesis 25:27-34). As a result, Jacob stepped into that place and you see his name written in the genealogy of Christ instead of Esau's name. If Esau hadn't sold his birthright for some lentil soup, instead of "Abraham, Isaac and Jacob" we would read, "Abraham, Isaac and Esau" (Matthew 1:2). Jacob longed for the birthright and successfully pursued it. Esau didn't care about it. He was more concerned with having his belly feel good for the moment. As a result of Esau's lack of love for his eternal destiny and purpose, God said, "I have loved Jacob ... but I have hated Esau" (Malachi 1:2-3). Like Jacob, the Bride's heart passionately pursues and embraces the call and, as a result, becomes the chosen. The Lord loves the Bride, for her affections are for Him.

The marriage supper of the Lamb is soon to take place and you, beloved, are called to this celebration as His glorious Bride.

At the marriage supper there will be the guests, attendants and the Bride and Groom all invited by the Father. The Scripture says that it is a blessing to be "invited" but, oh, to be the Bride and not just an invited guest!

Then he said to me, "Write, 'Blessed are those who are invited to the marriage supper of the Lamb.'" And he said to me, "These are true words of God." (Revelation 19:9)

May you enjoy being filled afresh with His excellent grace and goodness in this hour of preparation. May the fragrance of your love for your Bridegroom be that which separates you fully unto Him. May you be fully arrayed in His glory and His love in this hour. Arise and shine, beloved Bride of the King of Kings. YOU are His prize!

The Spirit and the bride say, "COME."

Revelation 22:17

Maranatha!

(Oh Lord, Come)

BIBLIOGRAPHY

Internet Research Material

(Note: These links are from 2010 when the material was retrieved.)

The Blue Letter Bible (Bible Translations, Lexicons, Commentaries)
www.blueletterbible.org

The Ancient Jewish Wedding Ceremony
www.laydownlife.net

Ancient Jewish Wedding Ceremony by Tara Hart
www.thetruthconnection.com

Jewish Marriage Customs by Dr. Renald Showers
www.biblestudymanuals.net/jewish_marriage_customs.htm

Yom Kippur
www.christcenteredmall.com

Feast of Trumpets/Rosh Hashanah
www.bibleprophesy.org

Ancient Jewish Wedding Customs
www.focusonjerusalem.com

Feast of Trumpets
www.bibleprophesy.org

Days of Awe, Judaism 101
www.jewfaq.org

Chuppah, Wikipedia
www.wikipedia.org

Tribulation, Wikipedia
www.wikipedia.org

Jewish Views of Marriage, Wikipedia
www.wikipedia.org

The Evolution of Marriage: Ancient by Hayyim Schauss
www.myjewishlearning.com

Like a Thief in the Night by Jennifer Rast
www.millmag.org

A Fresh Look at the Jewish Wedding
www.mayimhayim.org

Will Christians Go Through the Great Tribulation? by Rich
Deem
www.godandscience.org

DECREES OF THE BRIDE

1. I love my Bridegroom Jesus with all my heart, mind, and strength. (Deuteronomy 6:5-6)

2. With "dove's eyes," I am single in my bridal focus and have no other gods before Him. (Song of Songs 4:1; Exodus 20:3-4)

3. I am submissive, meek, obedient, and fully yielded to my Bridegroom King. (1 Peter 3:4-6)

4. The blood of Jesus has made me pure and beautiful, and I have made myself ready for Him. (Hebrews 9:14; Revelation 19:7)

5. As His Bride, I am clothed in righteous acts and like Him, go about doing good. (Revelation 19:8; Acts 10:38)

6. As His Bride, I am virtuous, industrious, trustworthy, courageous, faithful, and God-fearing. (Proverbs 31:10-31)

7. I passionately seek my Bridegroom and am continually filled with the fresh oil of the Holy Spirit. (Matthew 25:4)

8. I long for the return of my Bridegroom and am alert as I watch and wait for Him. (1 John 3:2-3)

9. I am His glorious Bride, without spot, wrinkle, blemish, or any such thing. (Ephesians 5:22-29)

10. As His Bride, I am an overcomer. (Revelation 3 :12,21)

About Patricia King

Patricia King is a respected apostolic and prophetic minister of the gospel. She is an accomplished itinerant speaker, author, television host, media producer, and ministry network overseer who has given her life fully to Jesus Christ and to His Kingdom's advancement in the Earth.

She is the founder of Patricia King Ministries, Women in Ministry Network and Everlasting Love Academy. She has written many books and has produced an abundance of resources on digital media. She is also a successful business owner and an inventive entrepreneur. Patricia's reputation in the Christian community is world-renowned.

To Connect:

Patricia King website: PatriciaKing.com

Women in Ministry Network: WIMNglobal.com

Facebook: Facebook.com/PatriciaKingPage

Instagram: PatriciaKingPage

YouTube: https://www.youtube.com/c/PatriciaKingPage

Patricia King Academy: EverlastingLoveAcademy.com

Available at PatriciaKing.com

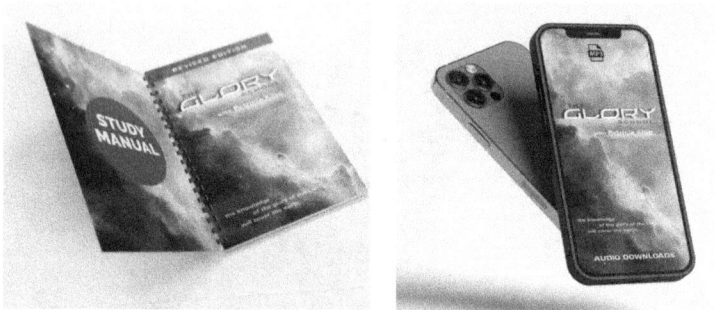

THE GLORY SCHOOL

Do you long for deeper experiences with God? Would you like to press in for a more intimate relationship with Him? Well, He is longing for the same with you!

The Glory School builds scripture upon scripture to guide you deep into the reality of God and His divine Kingdom. You will receive insight and impartation that strengthen your faith and deepen your relationship with the Lord.

You will learn how you can experience the angelic realm, the third heaven, and closer encounters with the Holy Spirit. Get ready to experience the Lord in completely new levels of revelation and intimacy!

The Glory School is available in both audio(MP3) and video (MP4) downloads and can be ordered along with the Manual.

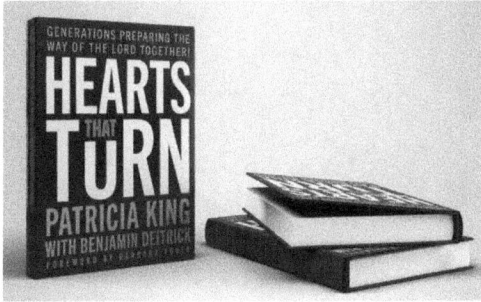

HEARTS THAT TURN

God's call for us today is for the generations to run together to prepare the way of the Lord. In an hour where there is a clear transition of eras, this call is more critical and relevant than ever before.

Packed with extensive biblical insight, an abundance of wise, practical counsel, and real-life stories and testimonies, *Hearts that Turn* shares:

- Key attributes of both spiritual parents and spiritual children

- The roles of mentors and leaders

- Keys for successful relationships across generations

- How to overcome relational hurt and fully experience God's fatherly love

Available at PatriciaKing.com

NARCISSISM EXPOSED

Tear down the strongholds of narcissism in your life or in the lives of those you love.

Many are held captive to narcissism. They are imprisoned by the deception of this wicked spirit and destructive mindset.

Patricia King delves into the psychological and spiritual roots of this disorder that is running rampant in both the world and the church. You will learn:

- What narcissism is and how it manifests
- How the deception of narcissism blinds
- How narcissism takes root in an individual
- The truth about narcissism in the church today
- How to overcome this rampant spirit called narcissism

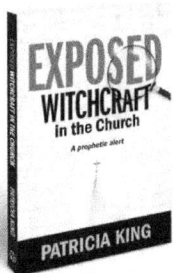

EXPOSED: WITCHCRAFT IN THE CHURCH

Witchcraft in the church? Yes. It is operating in the church today and many are suffering under its blatant and brutal assaults due to lack of awareness.

Patricia shares her personal journey with God as He has walked her through pathways of understanding, warfare encounters, and revelation on this subject. It is a prophetic alert for the Body, offering enlightenment and creating hunger to grow in God's Kingdom authority and to be fearless in the face of any adversary.

In Part One, learn about satan's strategies, including common witchcraft practices—and how to make sure you aren't inadvertently engaging in them!

In Part Two, discover your God-given power and authority over all the works of the enemy and 12 powerful spiritual weapons you have in Christ to defeat every device of the enemy.

Check out PatriciaKing.com for:

More Book Titles

Manuals and Courses

Downloadable Teachings

and more!

Bulk/wholesale prices for stores and
ministries are also available.

PKE

Patricia King Enterprises